Equestrian

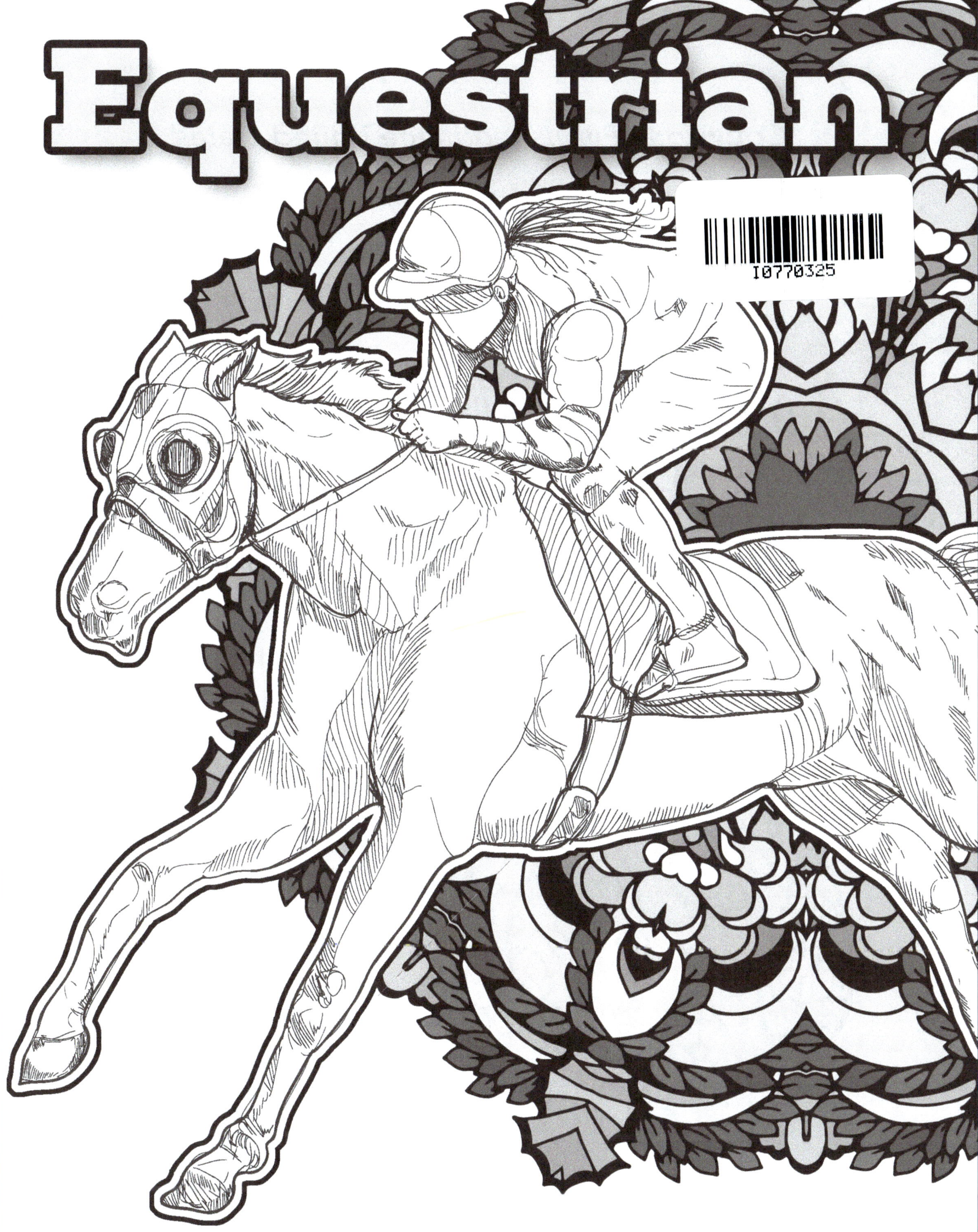

A HORSE COLORING BOOK

RELAXATION AND MINDFULNESS DESIGN

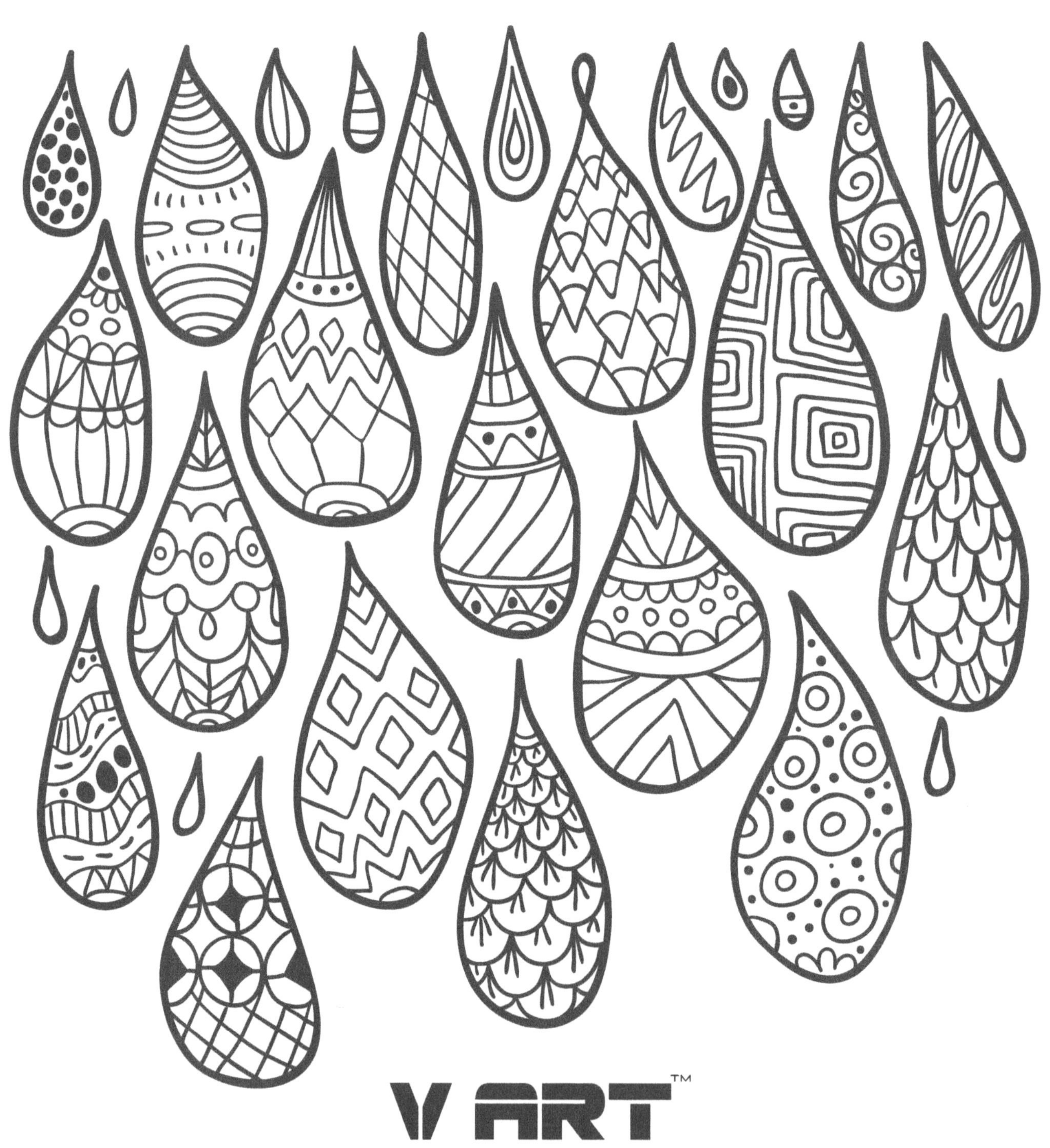

V ART™

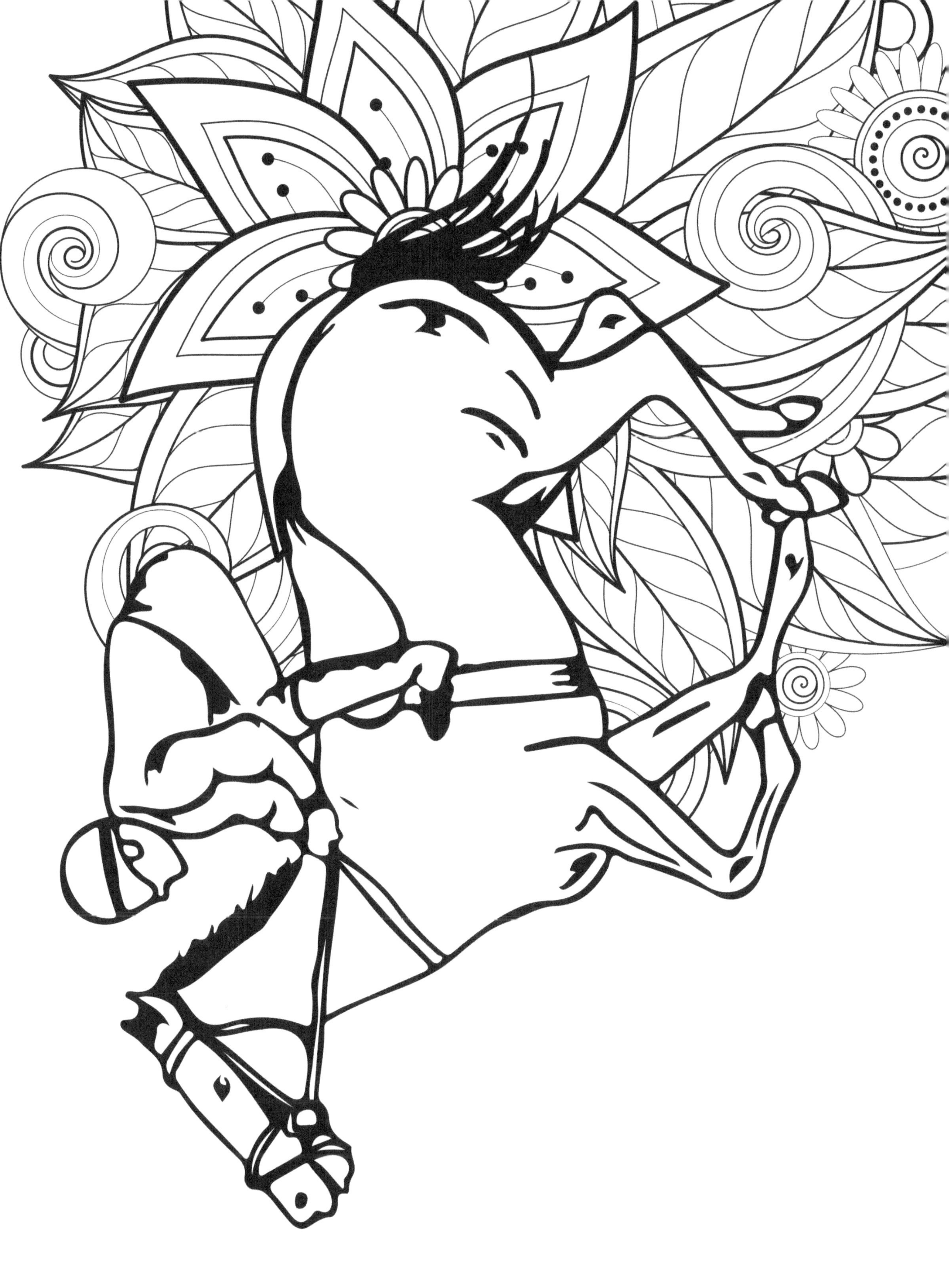

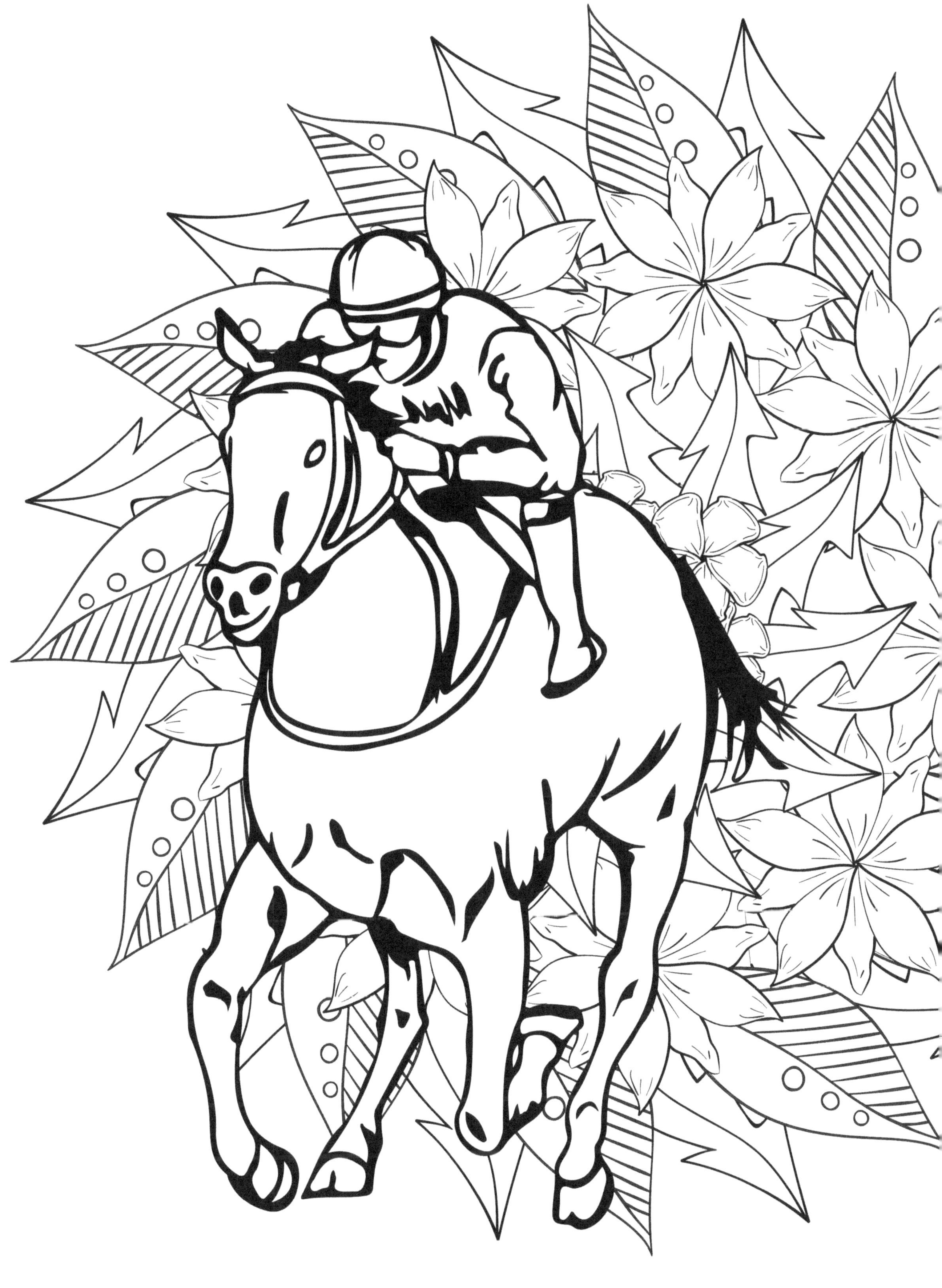

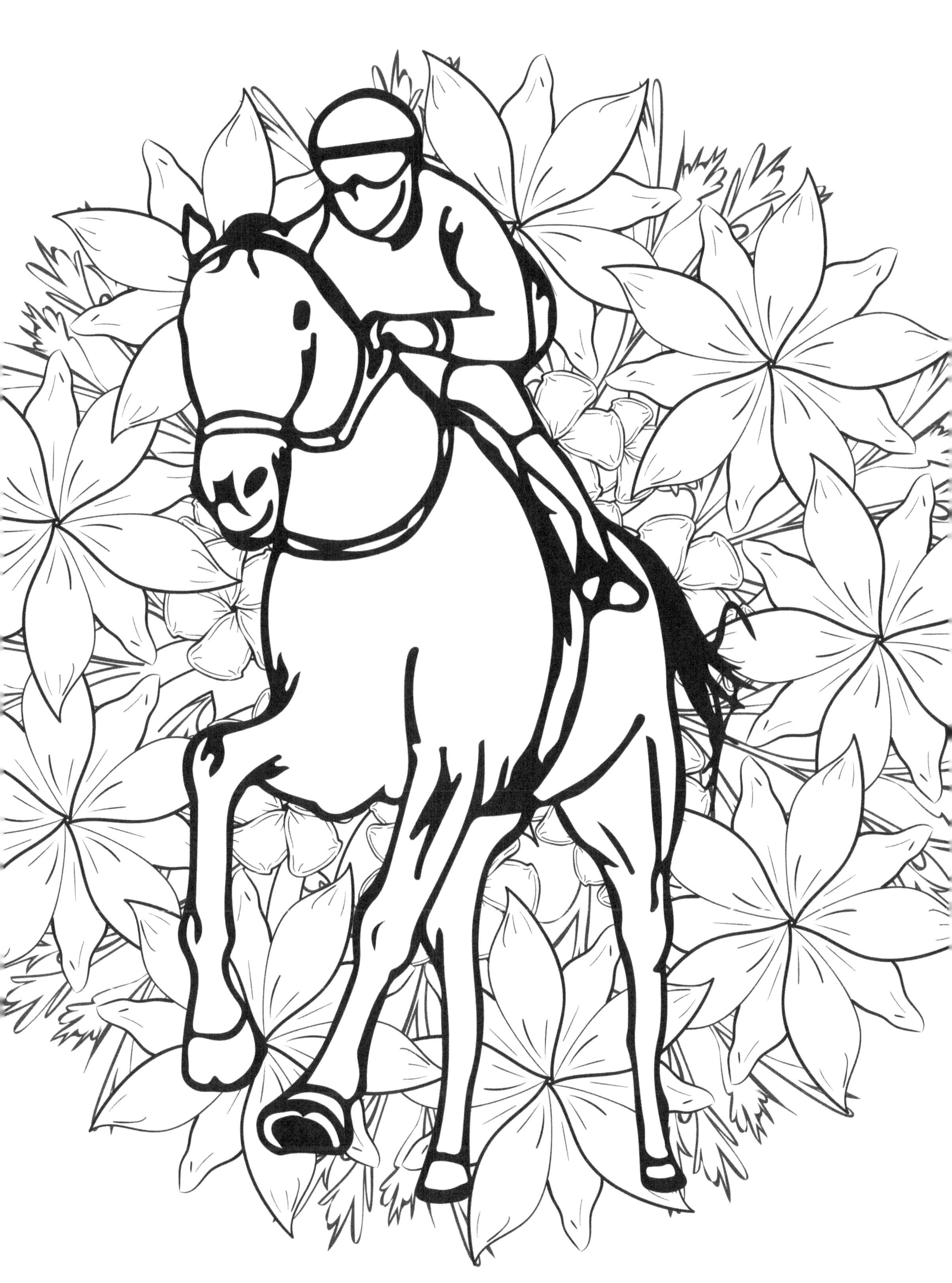

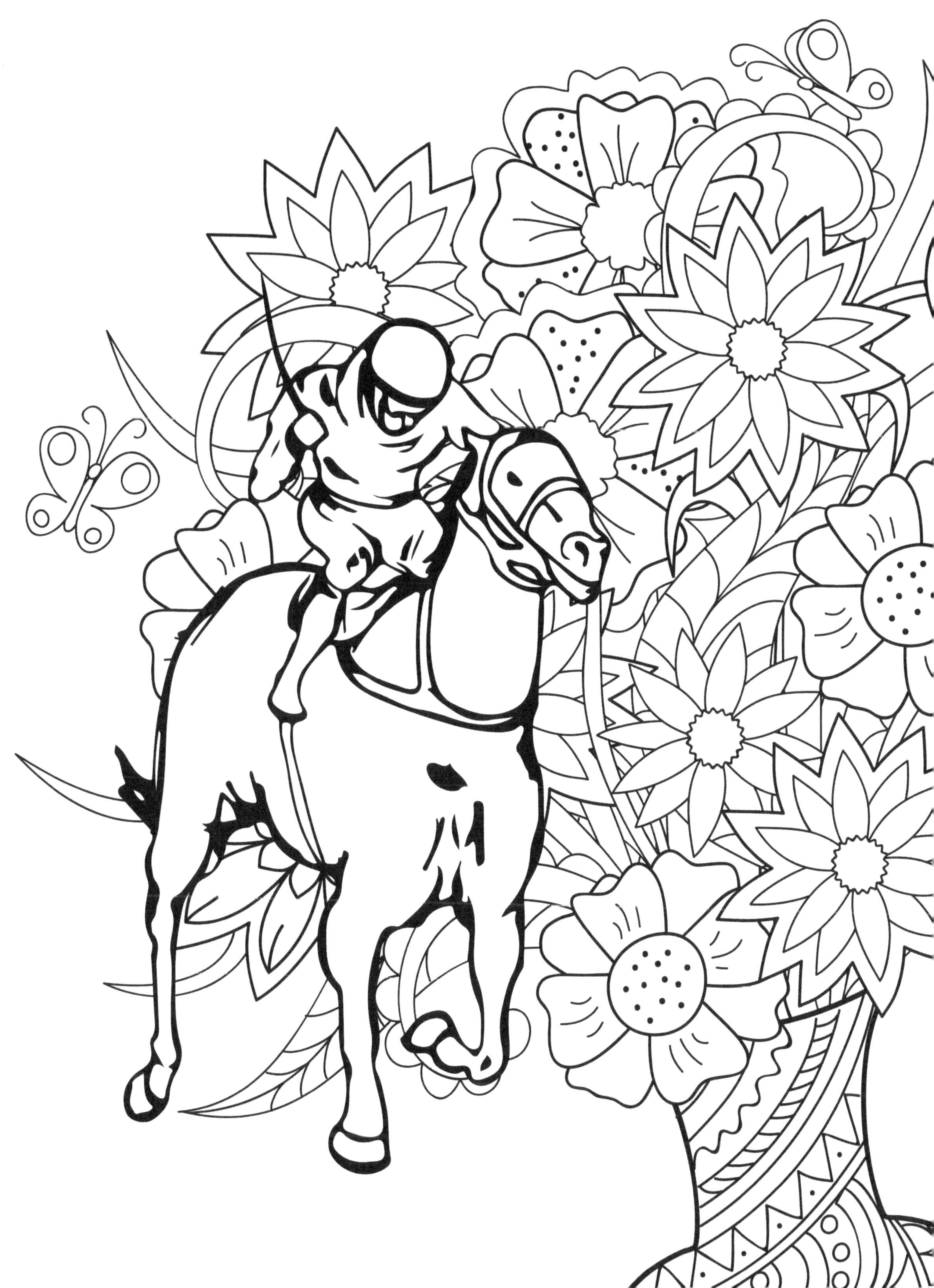

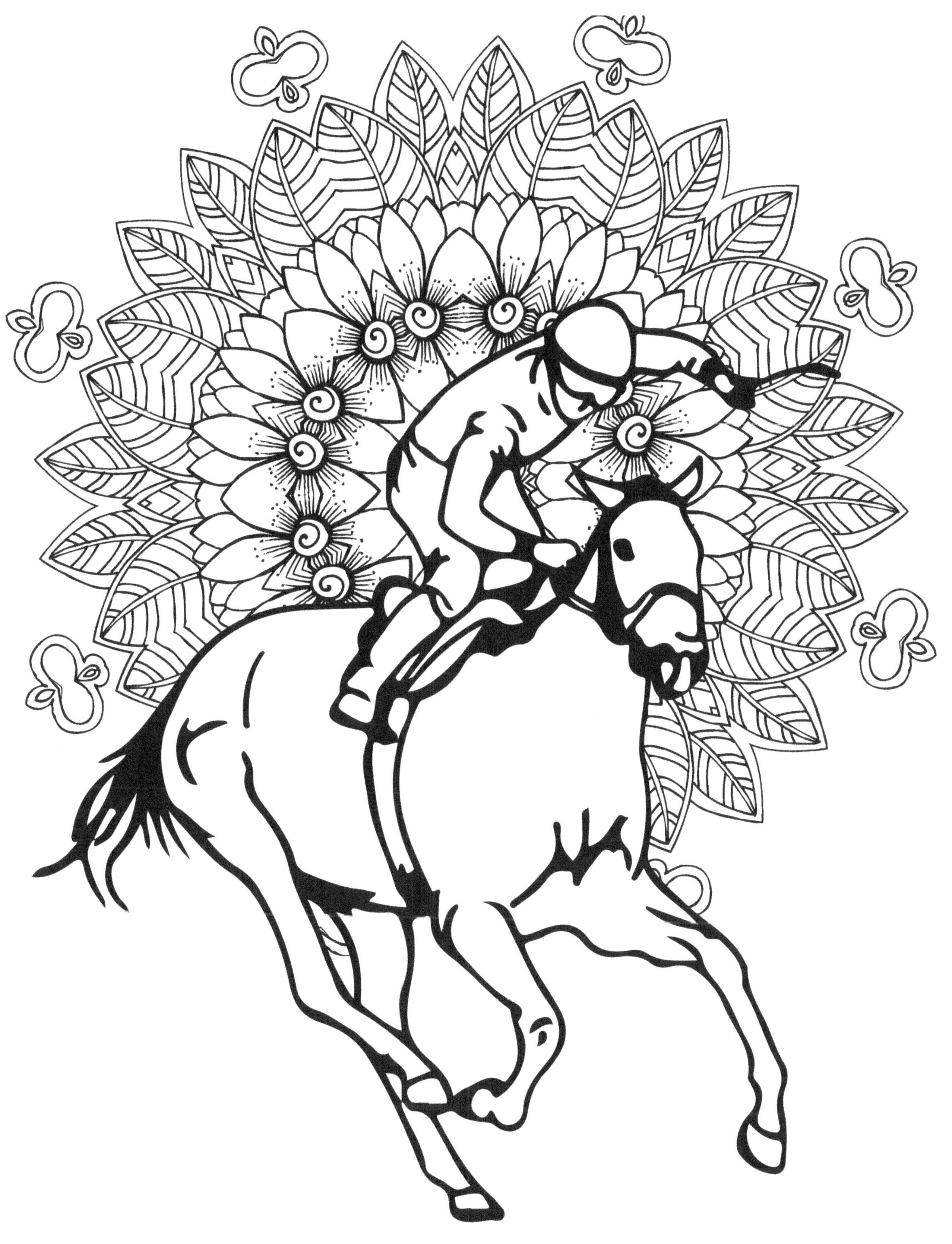

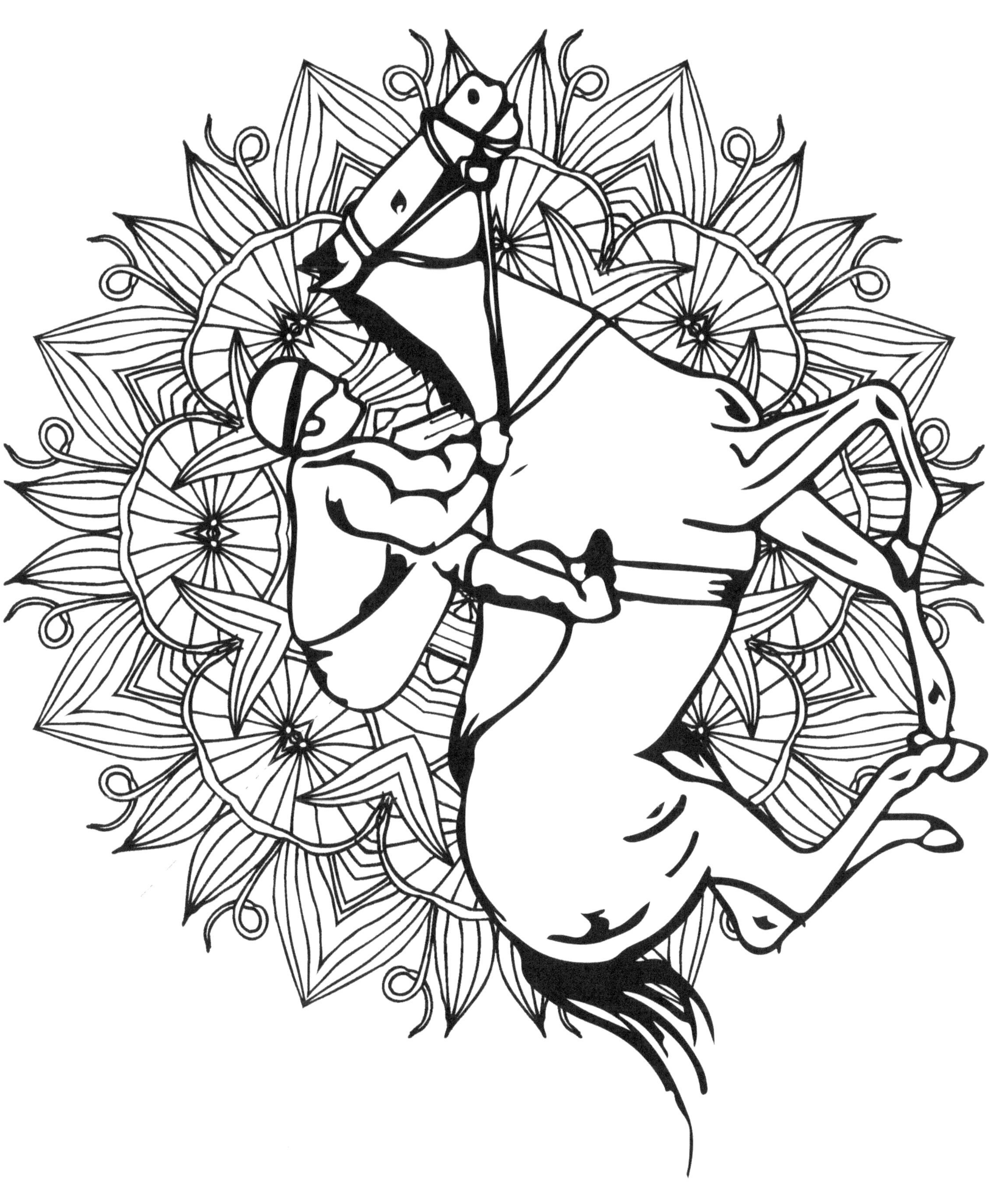

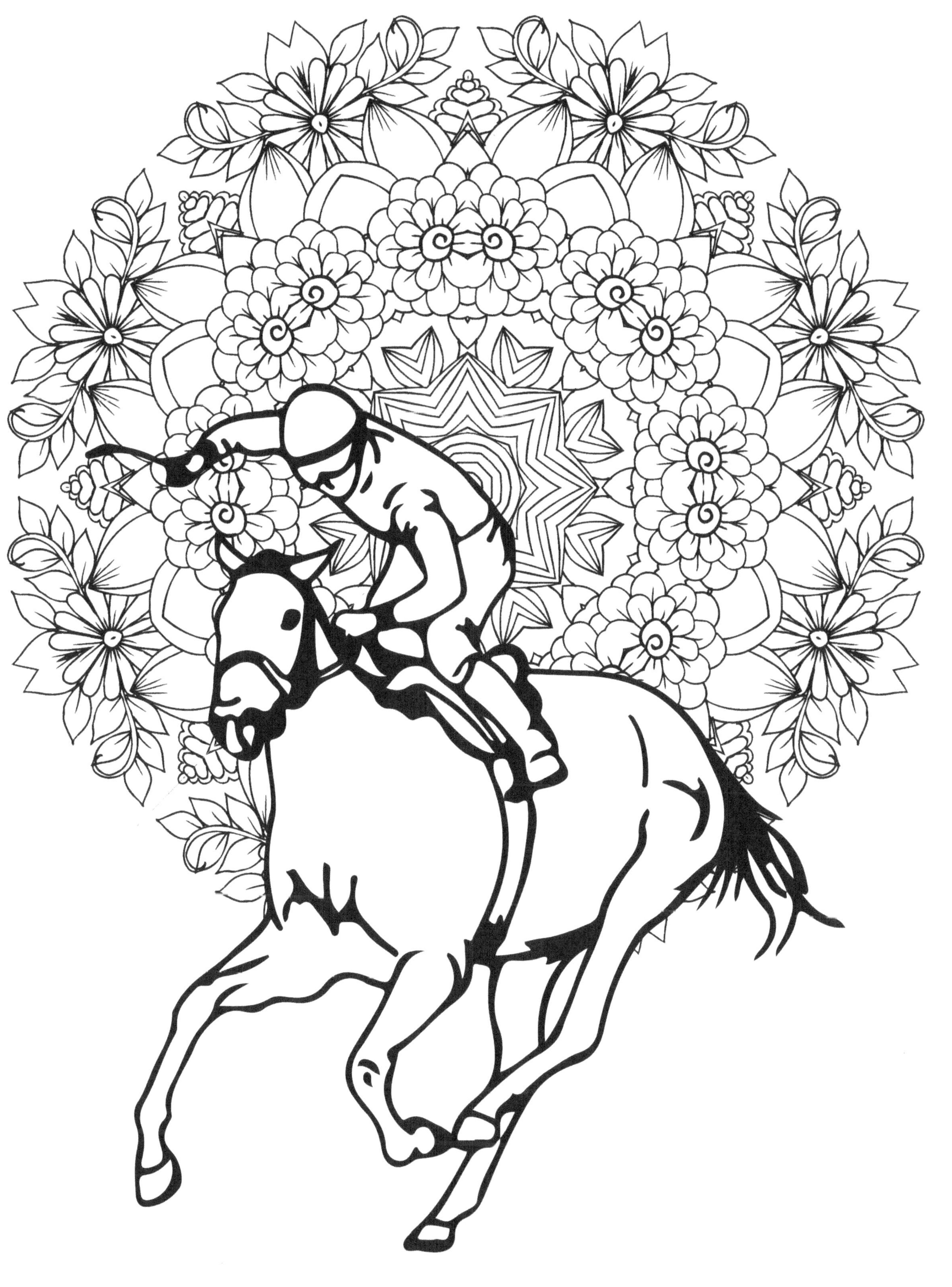

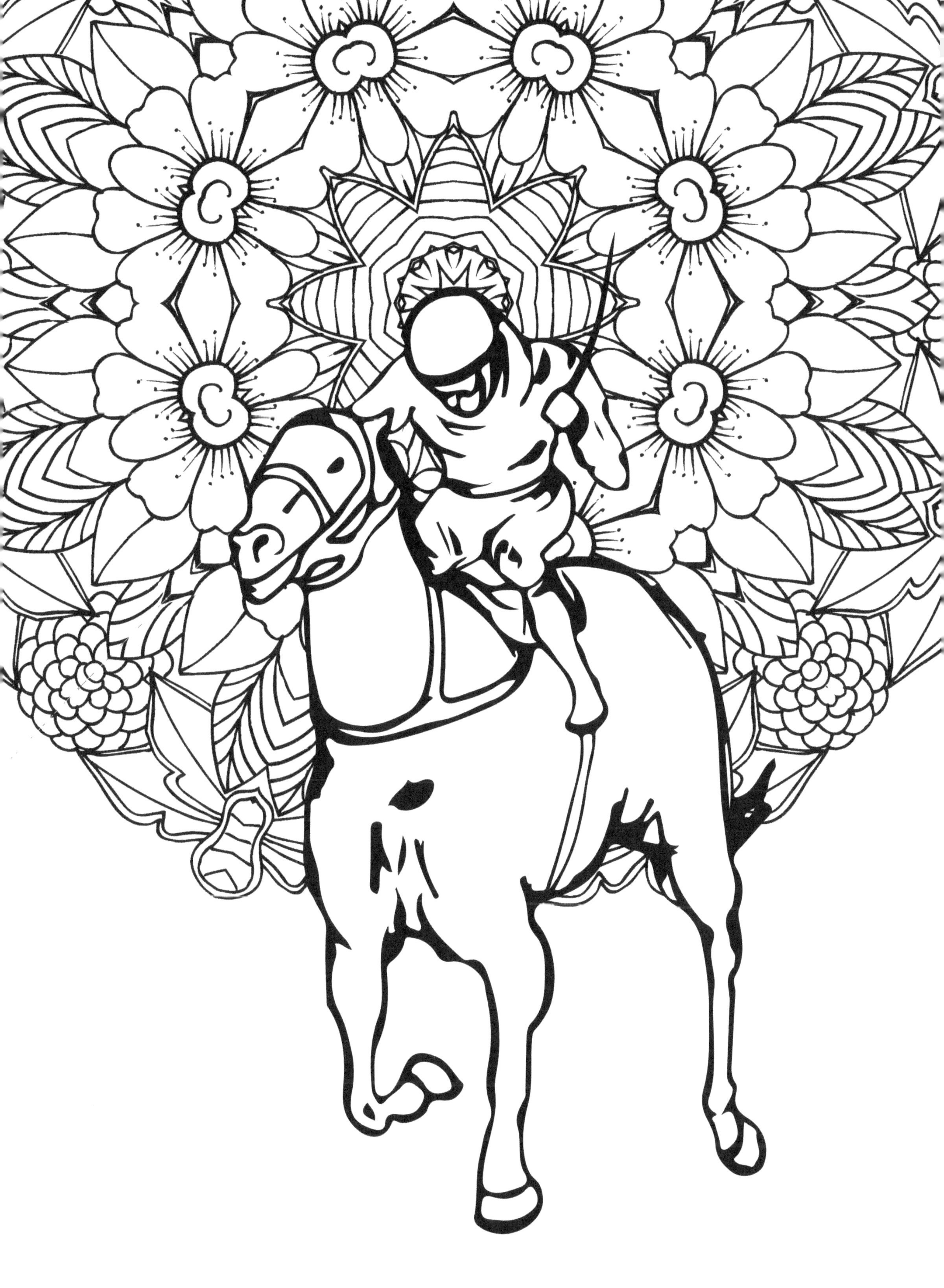

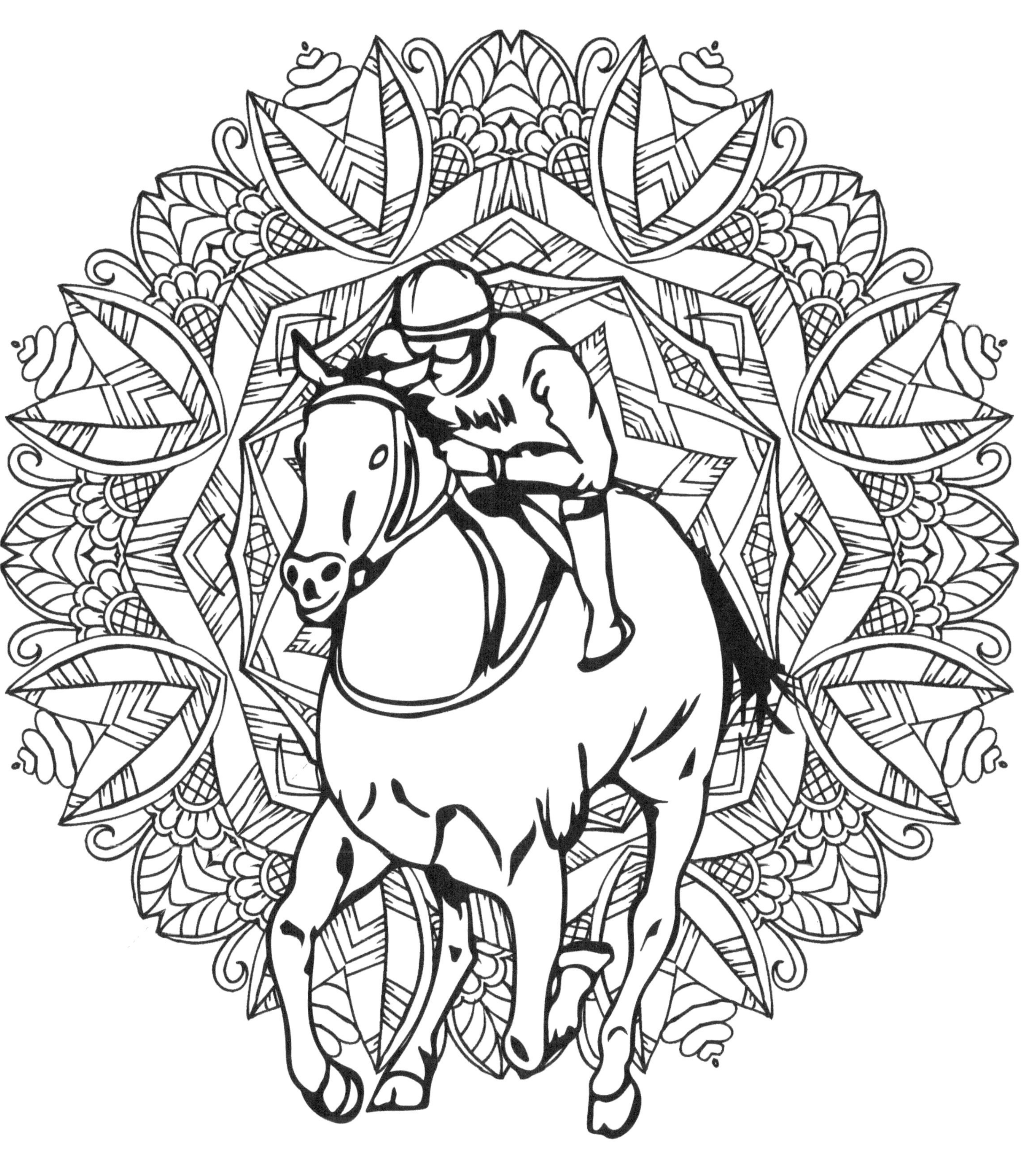

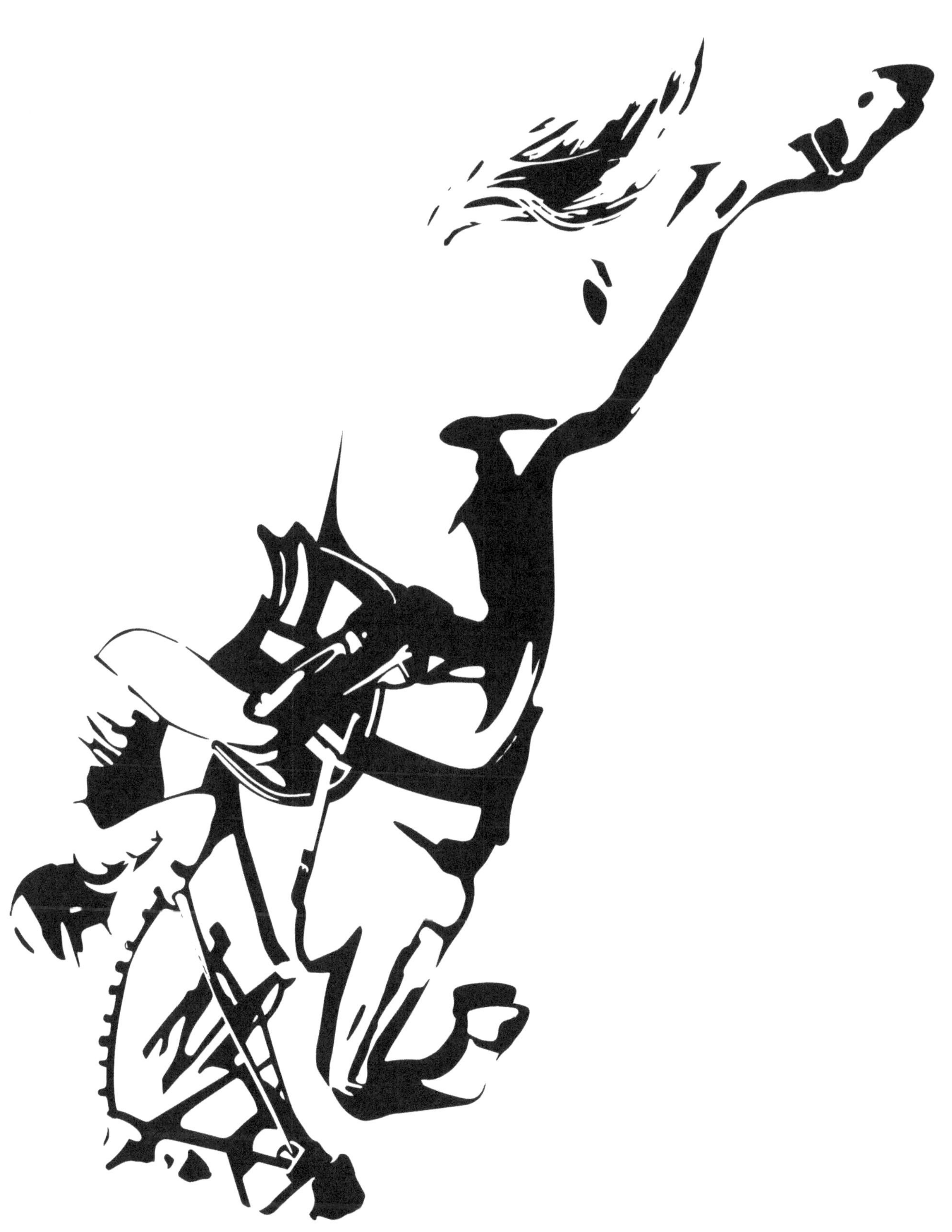

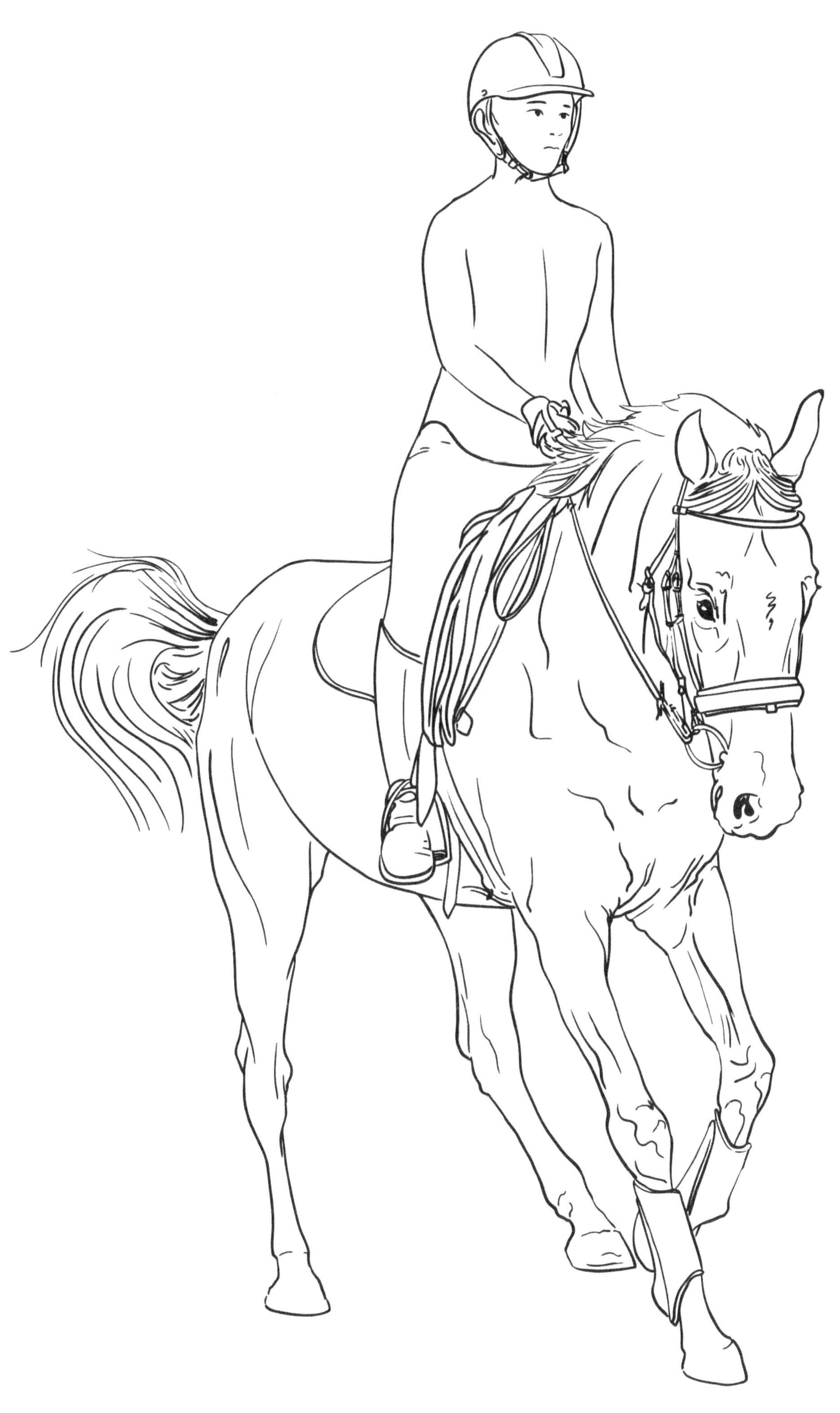

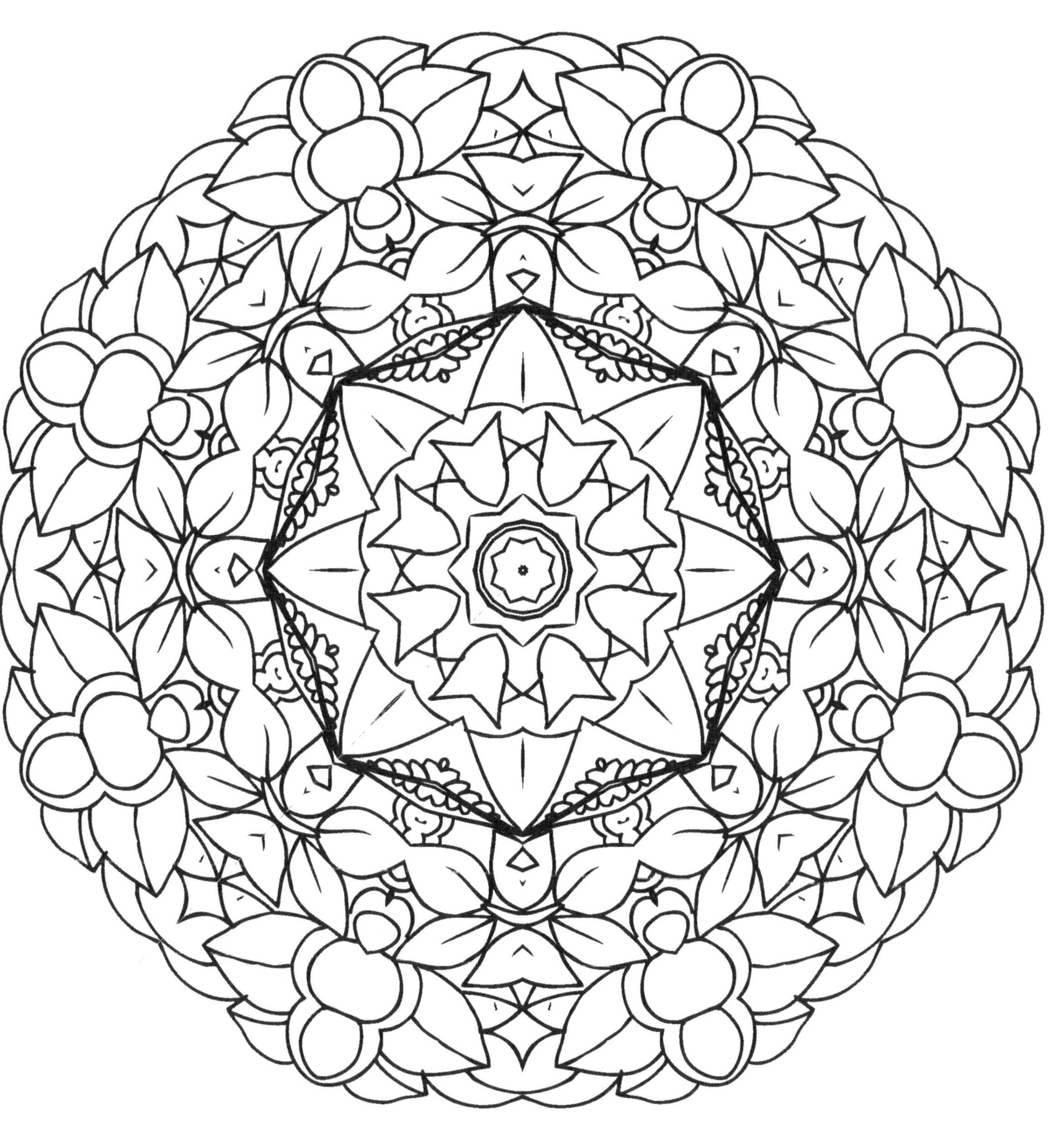

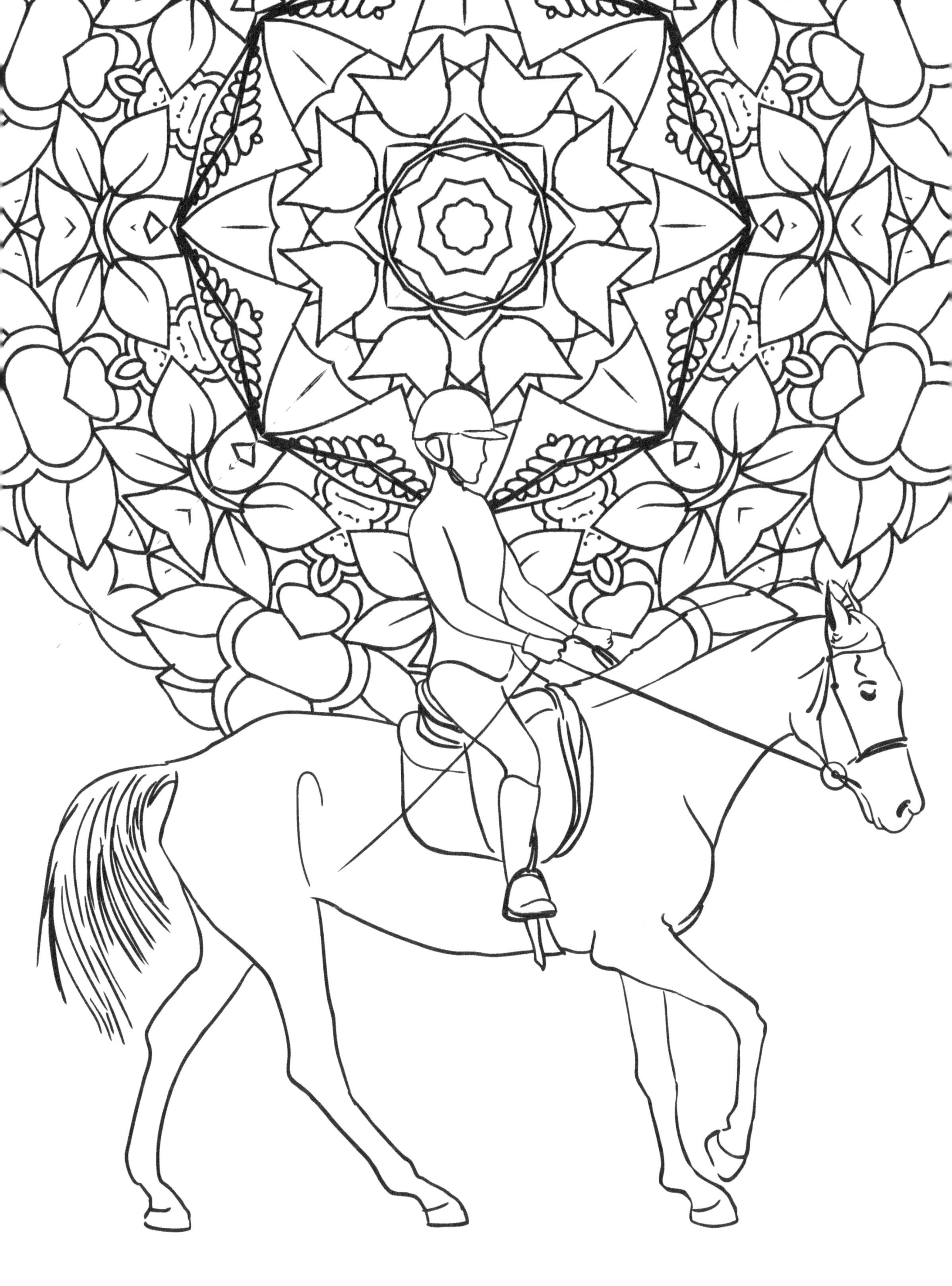

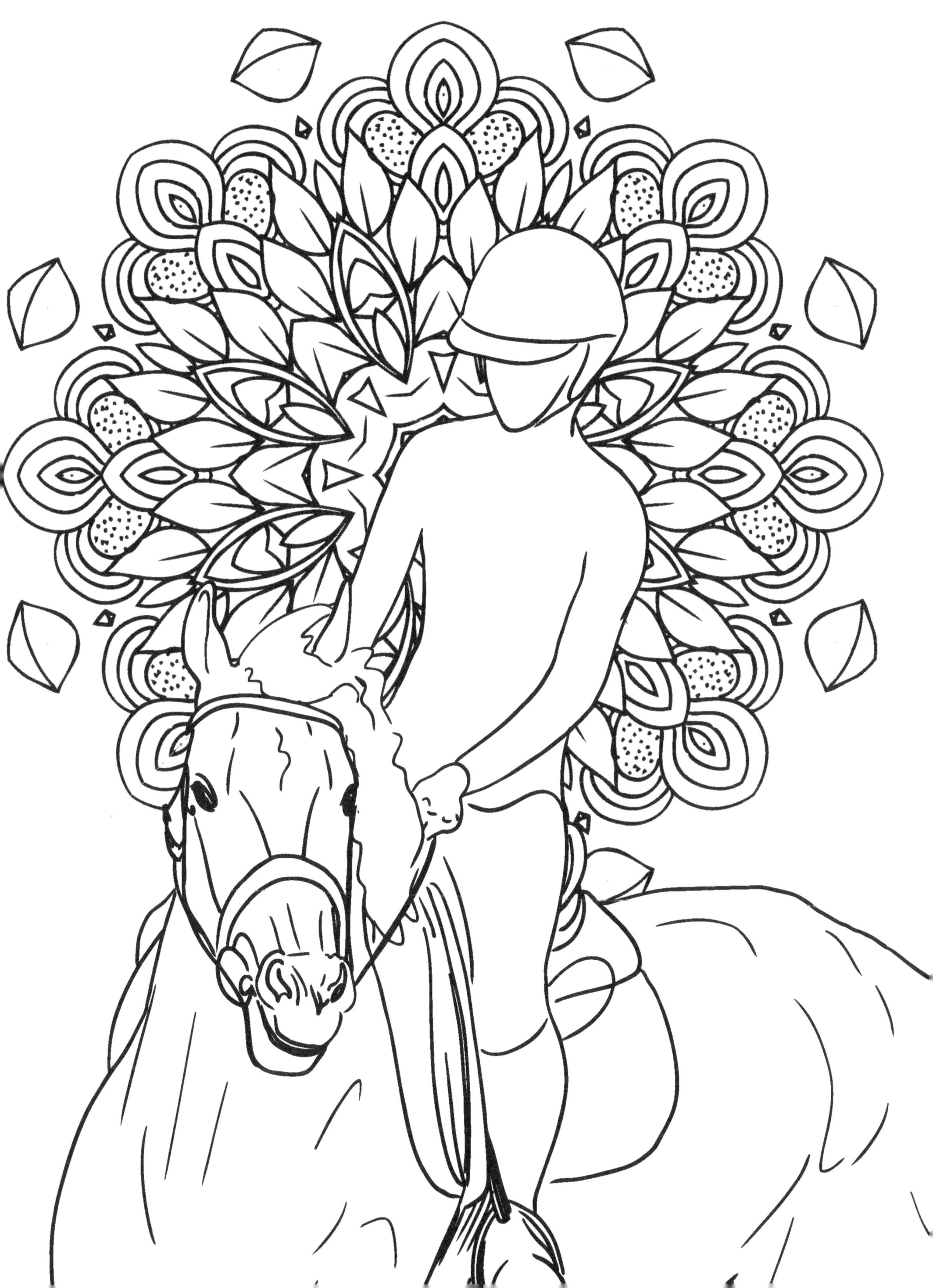

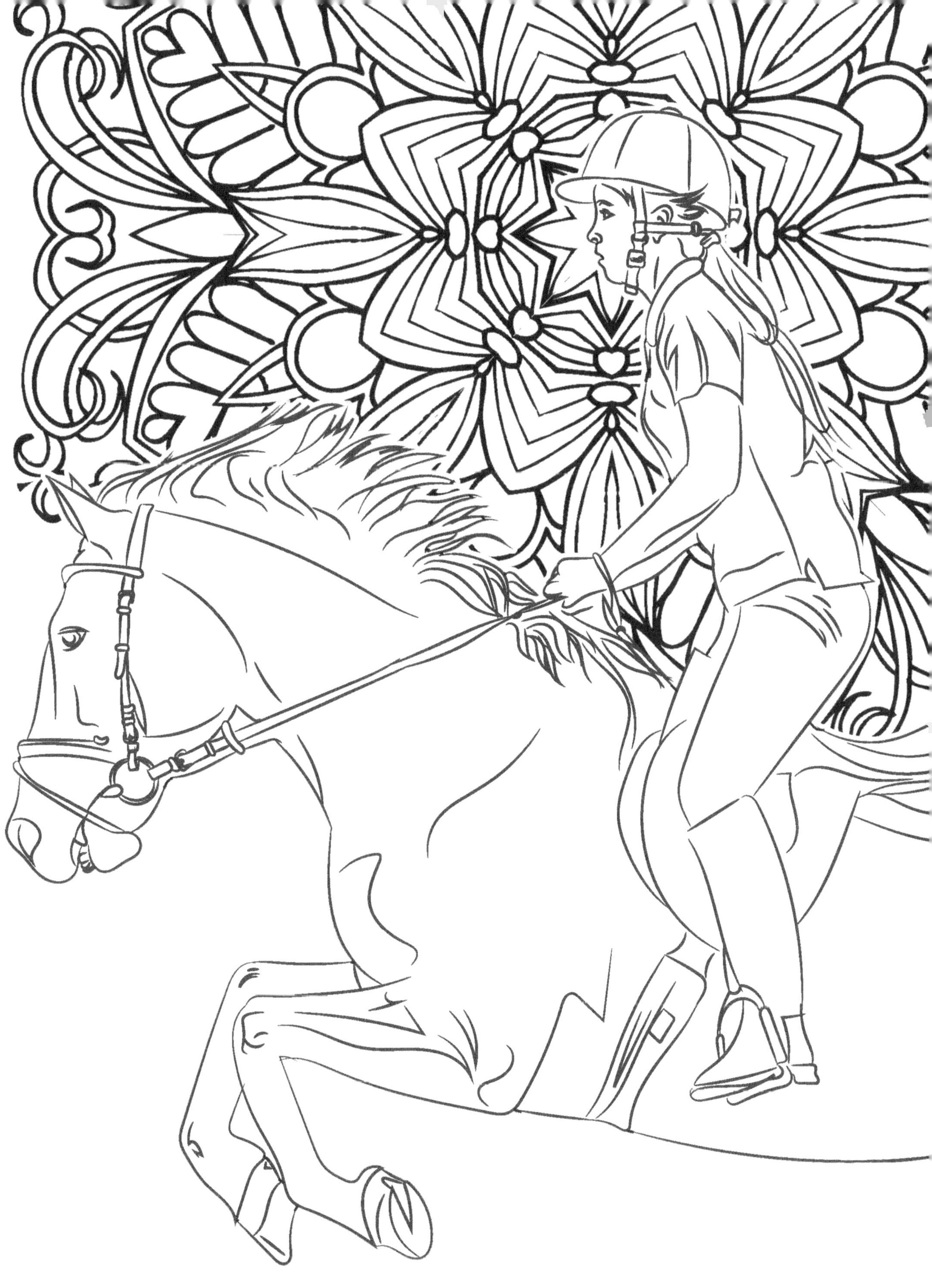

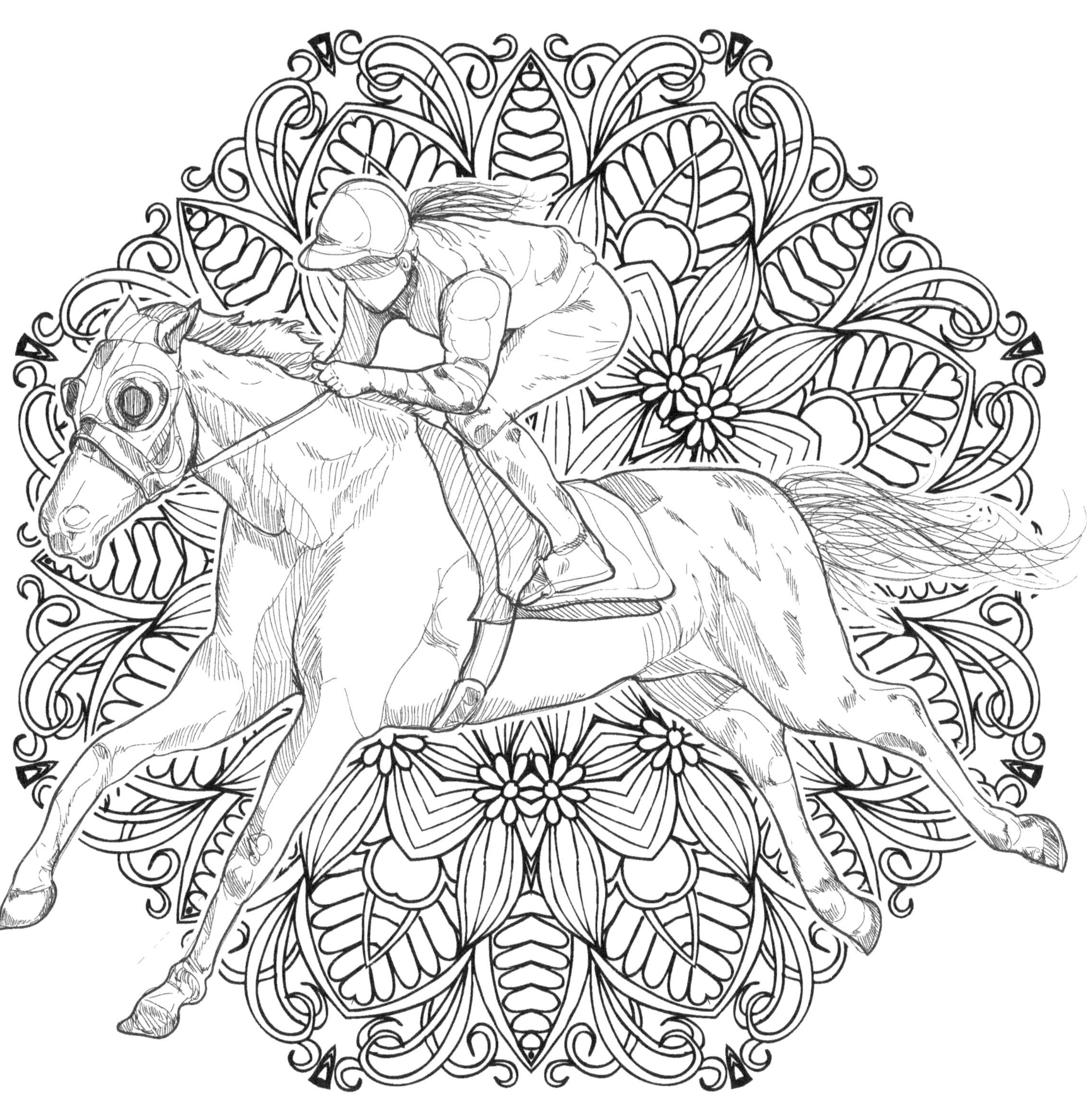

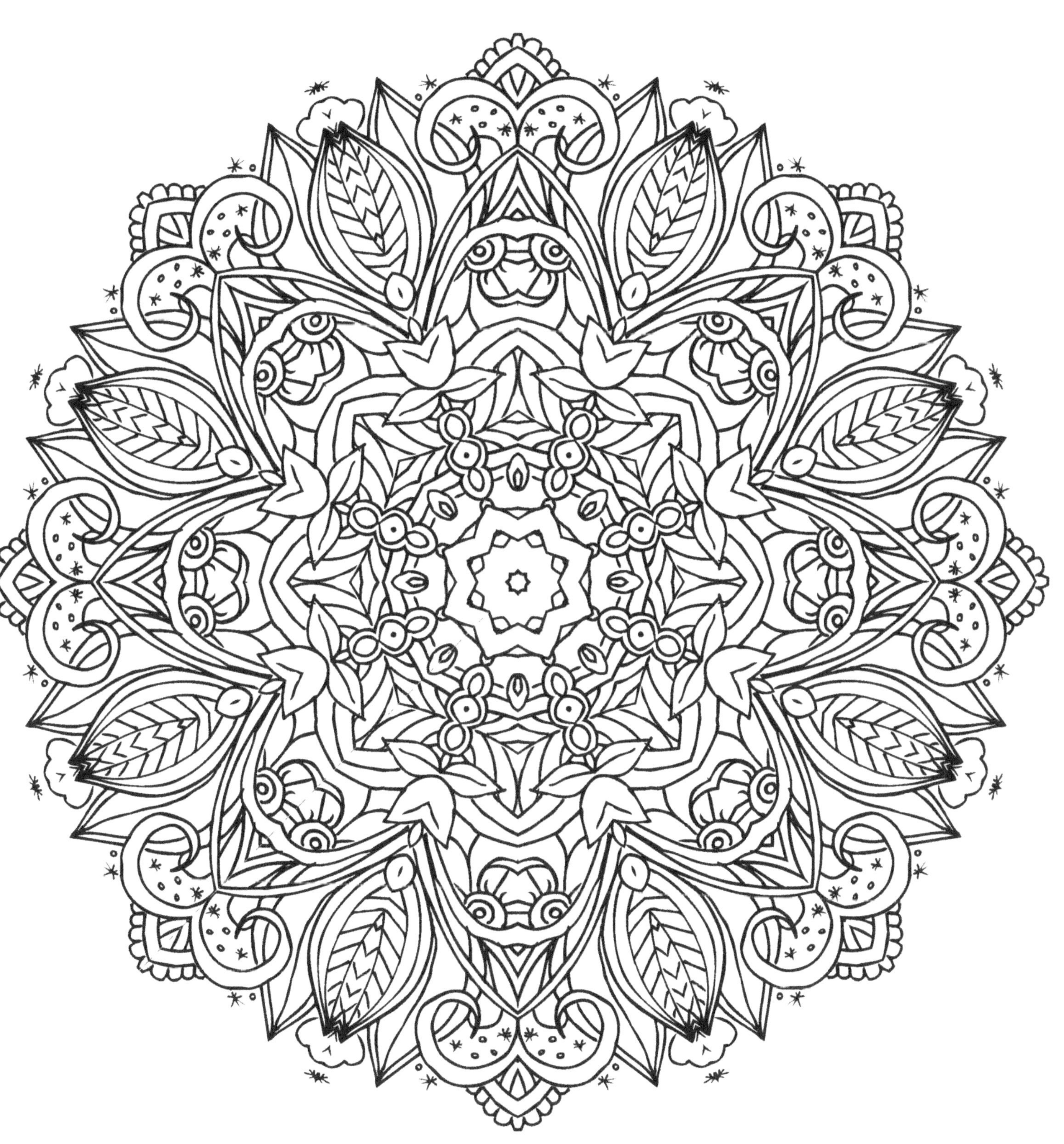

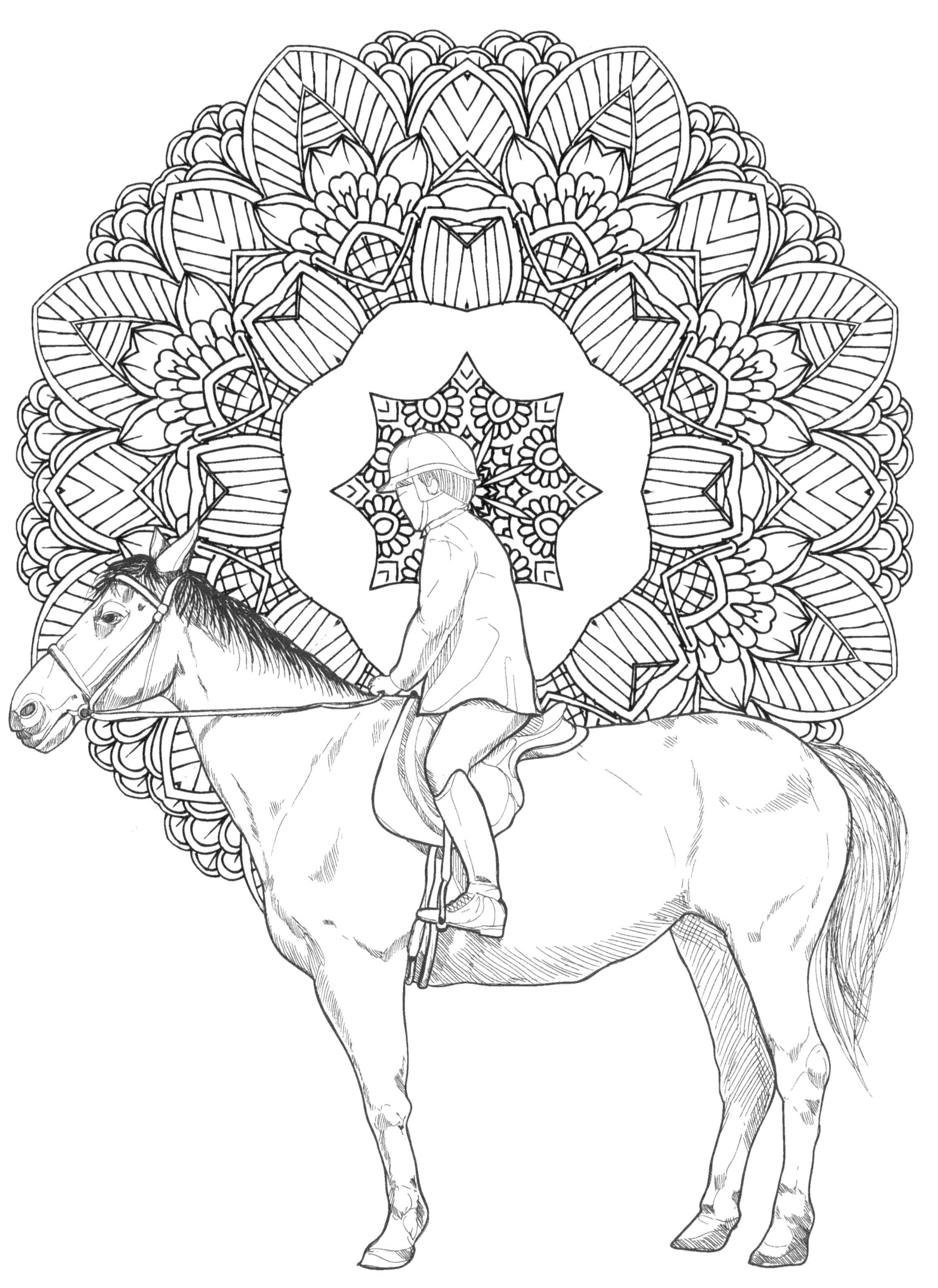

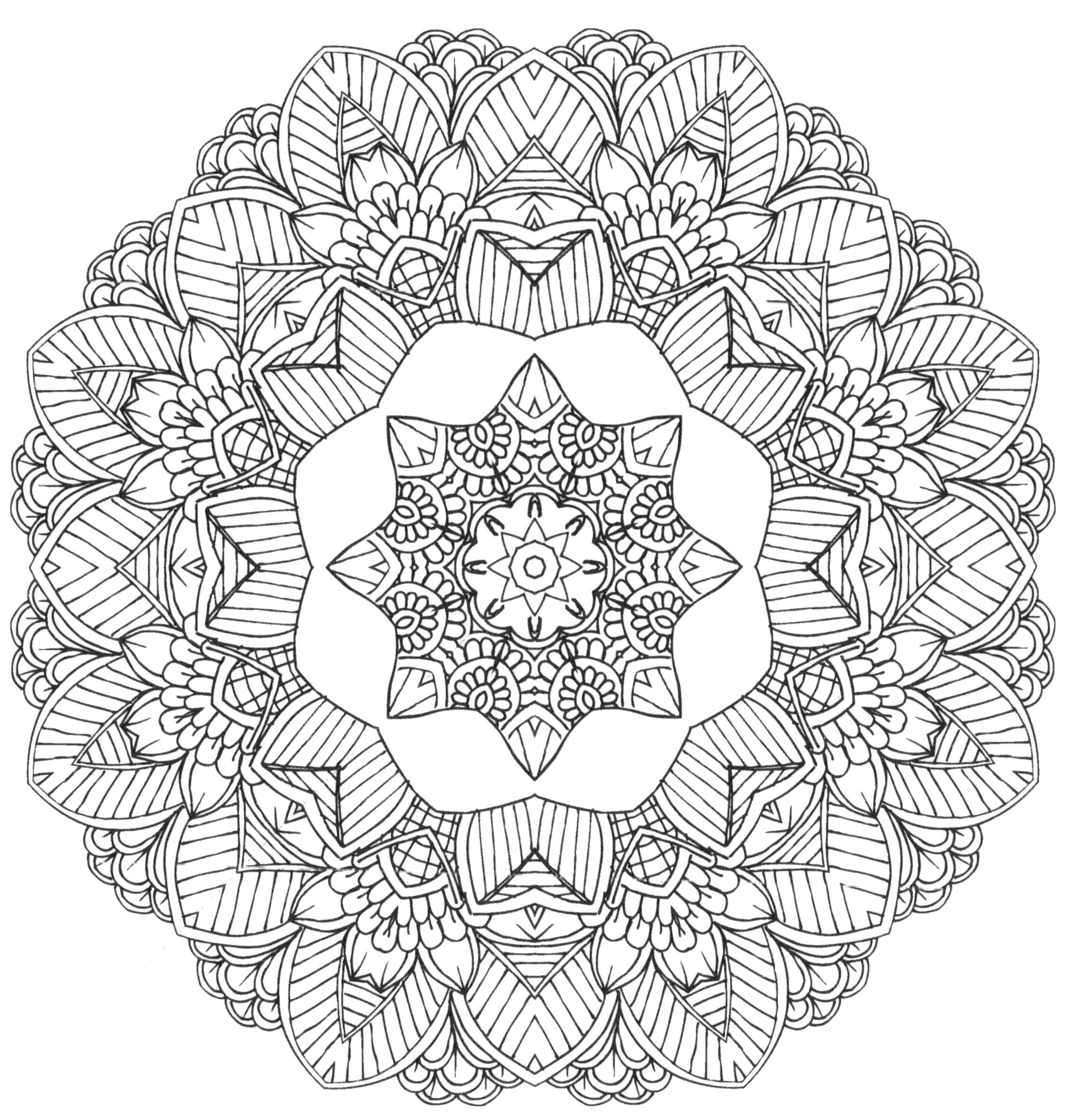

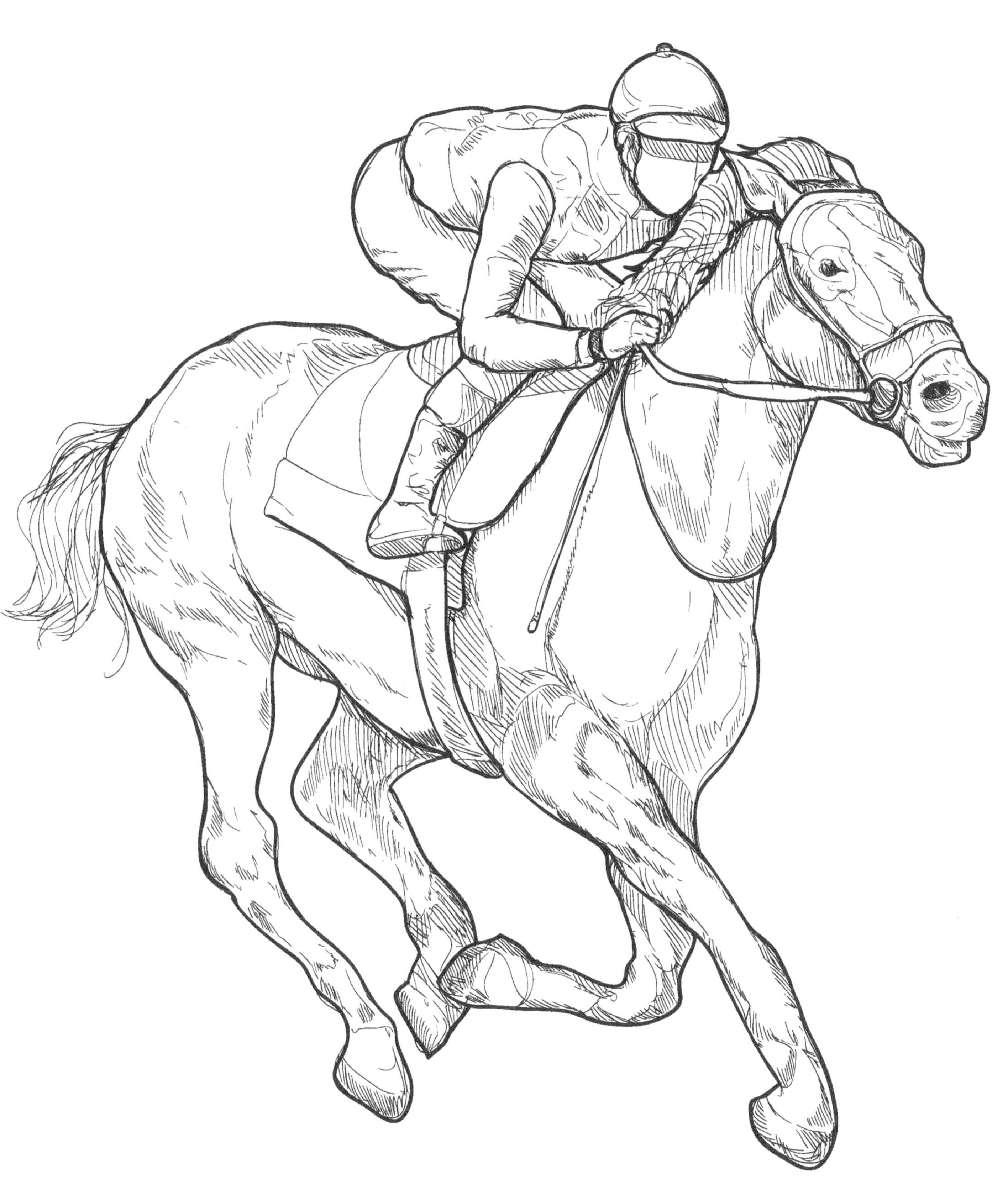

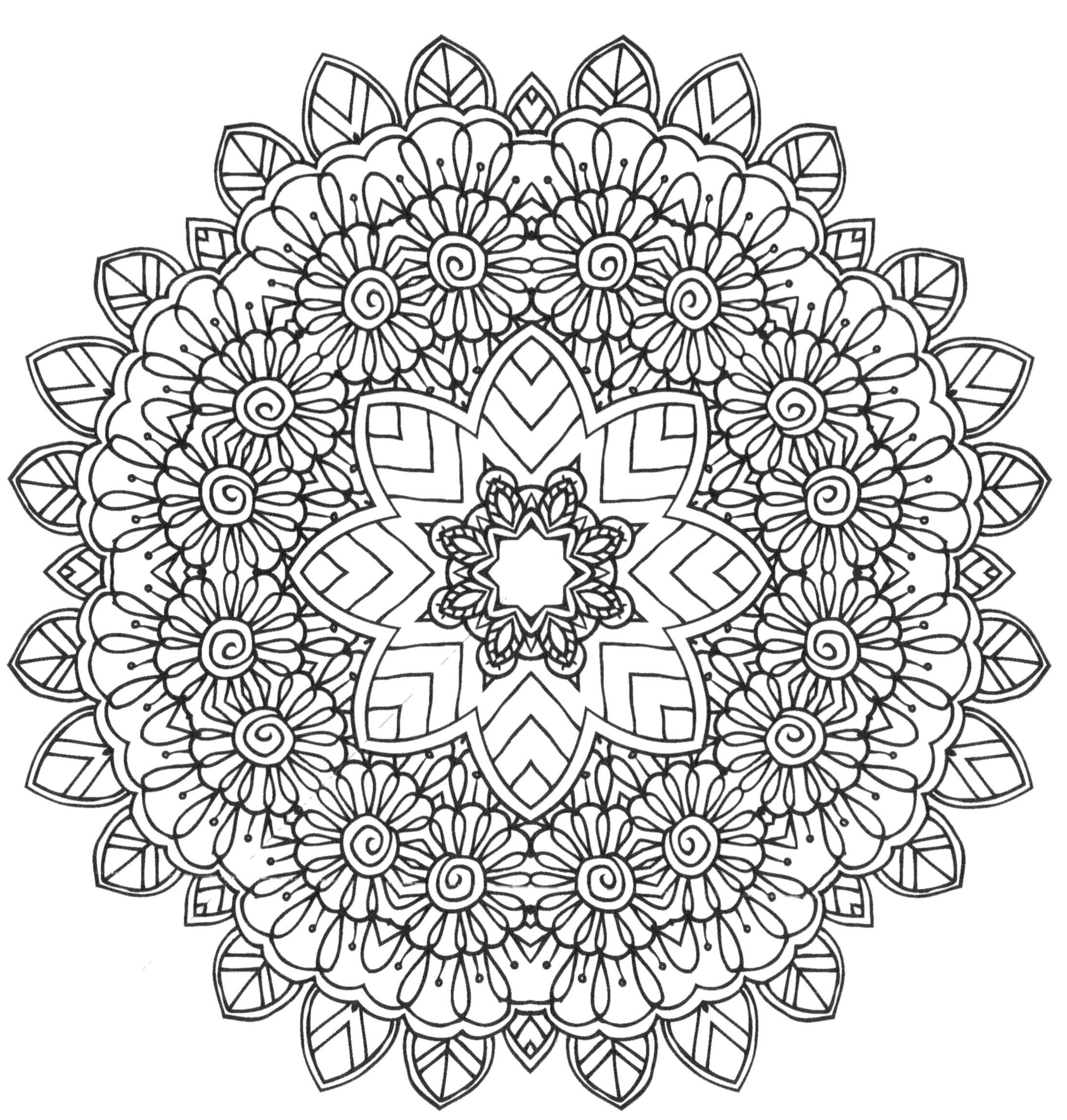

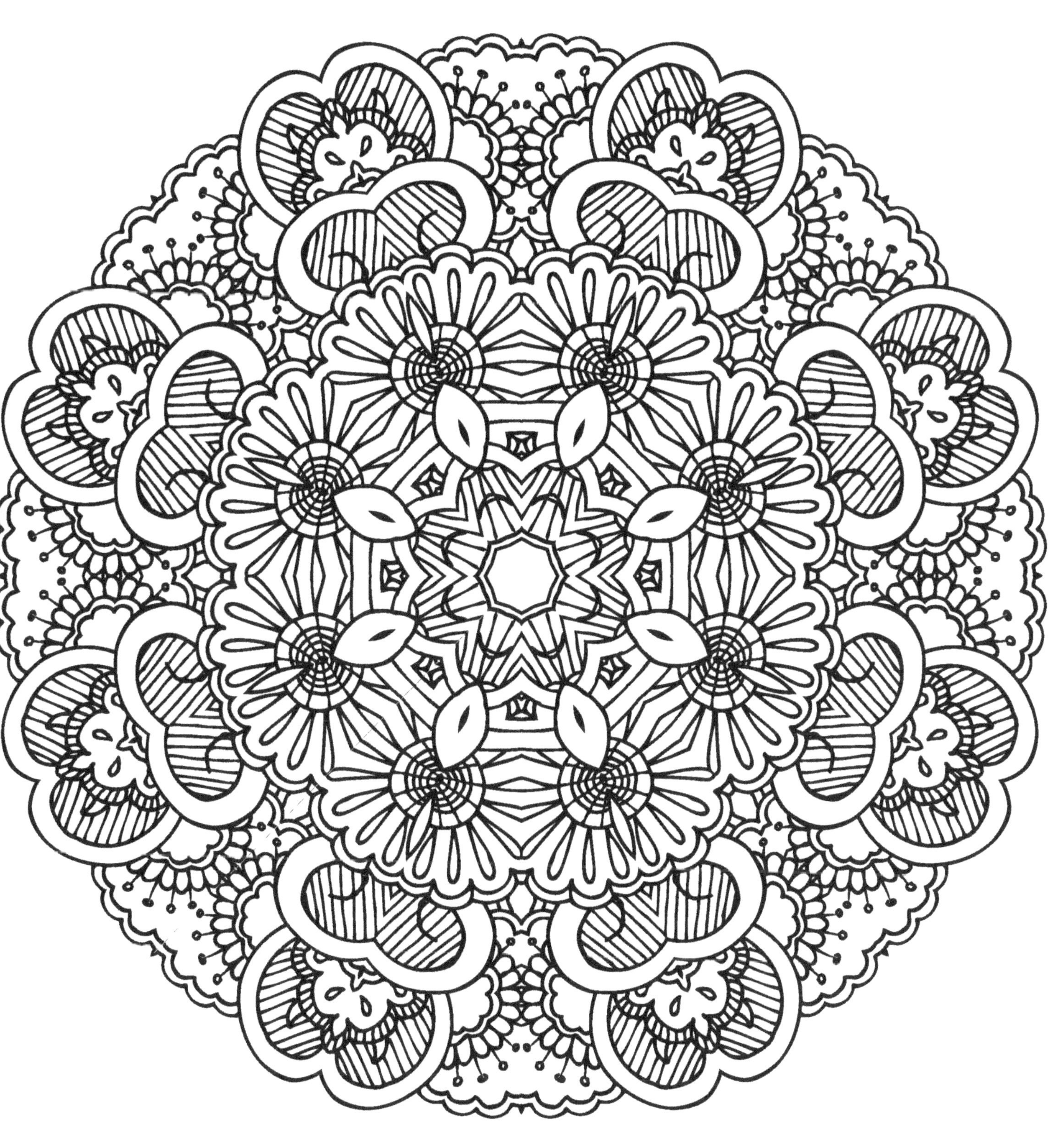

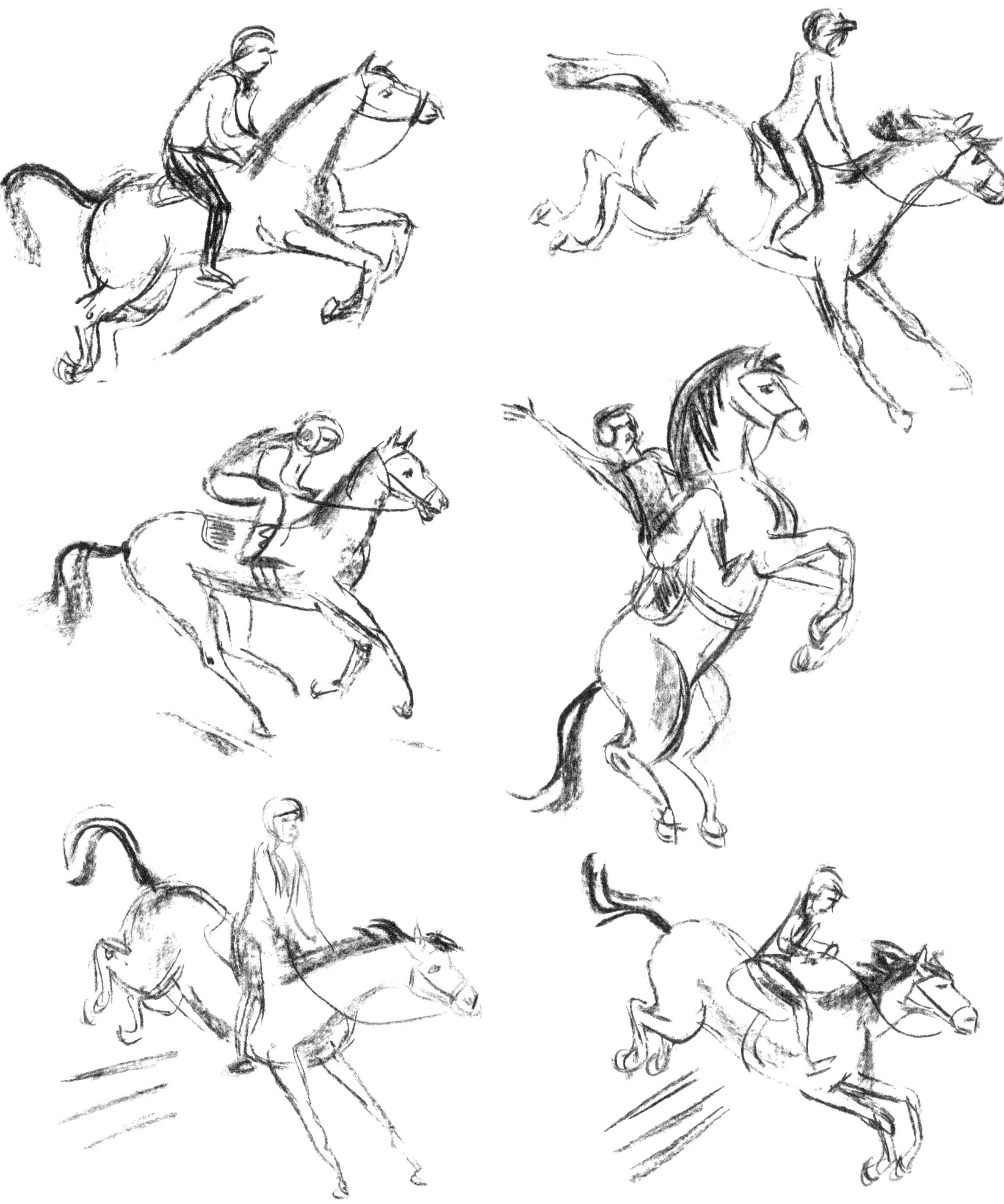

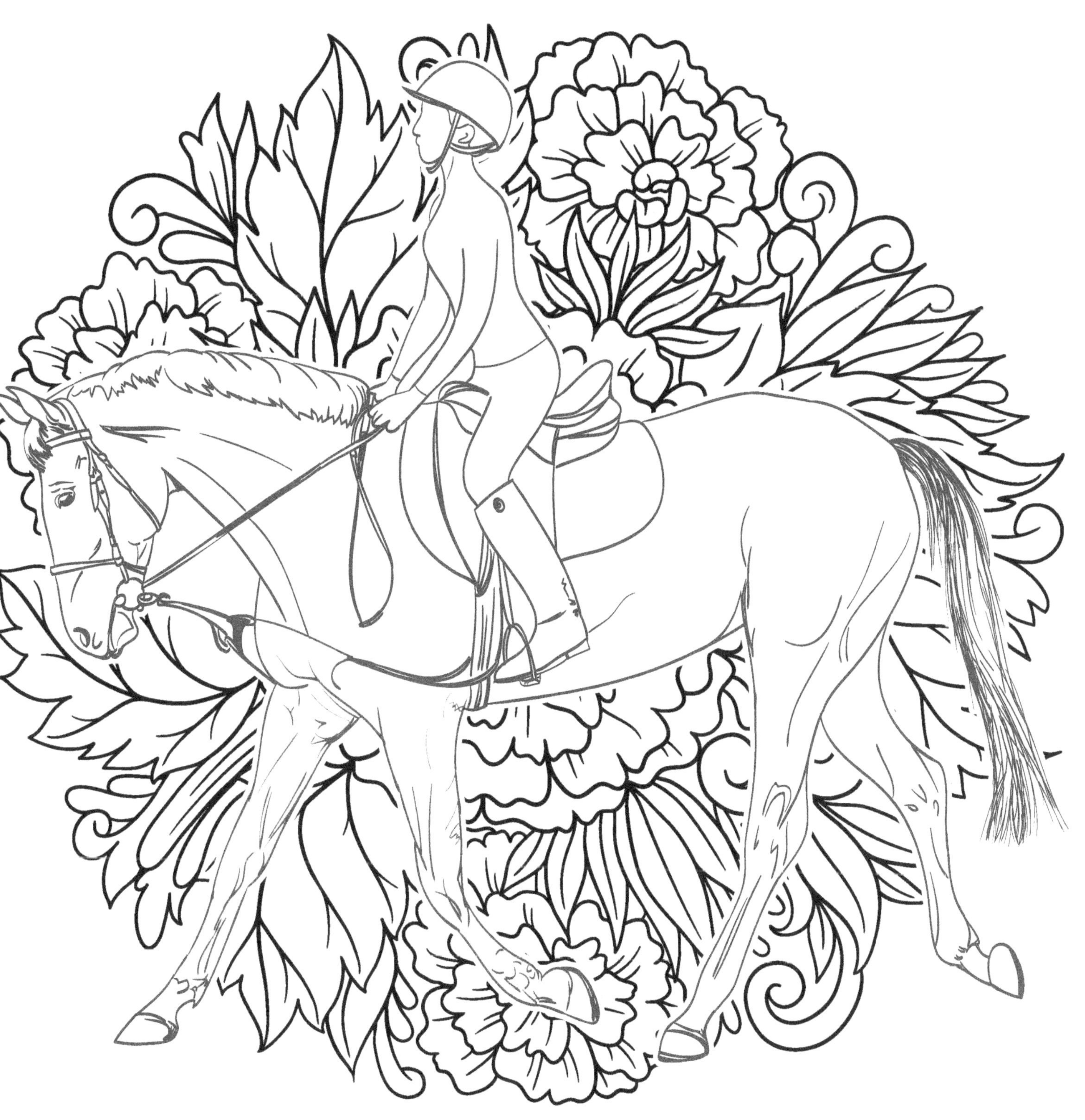

Parts of the horse

*Your Amazon Review could really help us.
Thank you for your support.*

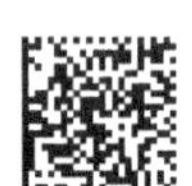